Glacier Bay

Glacier Bay

THE WILD BEAUTY OF GLACIER BAY NATIONAL PARK

ERWIN AND PEGGY BAUER

SASQUATCH BOOKS
SEATTLE

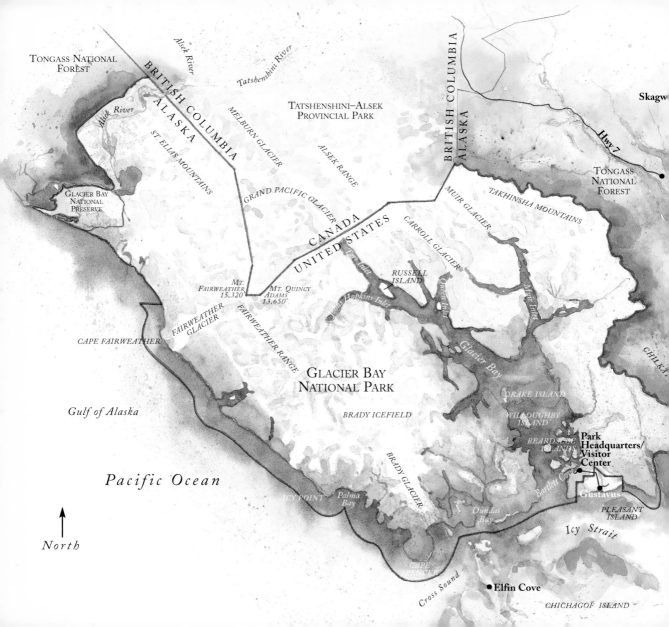

A Steller's sea lion stares at a passing boat from its haulout on South Marble Island.

During a career of exploring and photographing the national parks of the world, an exceptional few keep calling me back. One of these is Glacier Bay, a wild natural wonder in southeastern Alaska.

On my first visit there as a young man, I could not believe the strange, stark, and stunning wilderness scene I saw from the deck of a small fishing boat. Nearly a half

A sea otter swims on the surface of Glacier Bay.

century later, I still am awed by the great glaciers, magnificent wilderness, and abundant wildlife. Perhaps most remarkable of all is that Glacier Bay itself did not even exist 200 years ago.

In 1794, when English explorer and navigator Captain George Vancouver was sailing through Southeast Alaska's Icy Strait, in search of a northwest passage to Europe, he encountered a massive wall of ice at the present entrance to Glacier Bay. Stretching across an inlet now known as Bartlett Cove, this tidewater glacier was more than twenty miles wide and four thousand feet thick, presenting an impenetrable barrier to Vancouver.

The glacier that Vancouver encountered was a remnant of the "little ice age," which had begun four thousand years earlier. Prior to that time, much of the Glacier Bay area was ice-free, and members of the Tlingit tribe inhabited its valleys and shores. Over the eons, advancing ice slowly pushed the Tlingits out of their homes and hunting grounds. As early as three hundred years ago, Tlingits still lived in the lower Glacier Bay area, but soon the advancing glacier forced them to relocate to Chichagof Island, across Icy Strait. Not long after that, the glacier's forward movement ceased, forming the impenetrable tidewater wall of ice that stopped Vancouver.

In 1879, more than a century after Vancouver's visit, California naturalist John Muir, accompanied by Tlingit guides and S. Hall Young, a Presbyterian minister, arrived in Glacier Bay in a dugout canoe. The wall of ice that had forced the Tlingits across the strait and that had stopped Captain Vancouver was nowhere in sight. The glacier had receded. Muir and his companions paddled forty-eight miles up the bay, to what is known today as the Grand Pacific Glacier.

In the two hundred years since Vancouver's visit, the glacier has continued to retreat, sometimes as much as a mile a year, baring a seventy-five-mile-long natural treasure-trove of fjords, inlets, bays, and coves, and leaving behind at least nine tidewater glaciers and five major land ecosystems, all ringed by the Fairweather, Saint Elias, Takhinsha, and Chilkat mountain ranges. In 1880,

Mink hunt the wild shoreline.

U.S. Navy Captain Lester Beardslee named Glacier Bay and charted its waters for the first time.

Muir had come to the region to study glaciation and glacier regression, and he began what has become more than a century of scientific research on glacier movement and the regeneration of the post-glacial landscape. Other naturalists and researchers followed Muir. In 1890, geologist Harry Fielding Reid made some of the first scientific measurements of glacier movement. Nine years later, the Harriman Alaska Expedition, with prominent naturalist members such as Muir, William H. Dall, George B. Grinnell, G. K. Gilbert, C. Keeler, John Burroughs, C. Hart Merriam, and photographer Edward Curtis, visited Glacier Bay. Their observations and writings confirmed the scientific value of the region. In 1916, University of Minnesota ecologist William Cooper began plant succession studies and also began lobbying to have the area protected. In 1925, President Calvin Coolidge established Glacier Bay National Monument, and in 1939, Franklin Roosevelt doubled its size by proclamation. In 1980 this spectacular setting was designated a national park and preserve, most of its 3.3 million acres protected as wilderness.

In late spring of 1999, I traveled the length of this bay that had been an ice sheet only two centuries earlier. Rather than a sailing ship or dugout canoe, my vessel was a modern eco-tour catamaran. As it drifted below the Margerie Glacier at the head of Tarr Inlet, I watched in awe as tons of ice broke away from the glacier—calving it's called—and crashed into the inlet. A few harbor seals hauled out on the largest icebergs did not mind the thunder of breaking ice, but did eye us warily. A bald eagle and a platoon of noisy gulls landed on a huge blue berg nearby. Suddenly the sun burned through a morning-long overcast, and just to the west, 15,320-foot Mount Fairweather towered into view, looming over a chain of other great peaks. I and my twenty fellow passengers fell silent, marveling at a panorama unlike any other on earth.

To reach Margerie Glacier by noon, our boat had departed Bartlett Cove, near Glacier Bay park headquarters, shortly after daybreak. A river otter was already fishing from the wooden dock as the catamaran pulled out. A school of harbor porpoises appeared and seemed to escort us northward until a pod of humpback whales surfaced just ahead of us. Within an hour, the catamaran was idling just east of South Marble Island, which (next to calving glaciers) must be the noisiest place in Glacier Bay.

Thousands of black-legged kittiwakes, glaucous-winged gulls, pelagic cormorants, common murres, and other seabirds were nesting on the ground and in cliff rookeries. What a din they made as they circled above and around us! Birders on board also spotted tufted puffins, pigeon guillemots, red-throated and common loons, white-winged scoters, and the mysterious marbled murrelet nearby. (Although murrelets are frequently seen in Glacier Bay, no nests of either the marbled or Kittlitz's murrelet have ever been found in the park.) The loudest "welcome," however, came from the herd of Steller's sea lions, hauled out in a restless, seething mass on the steep rocky shore. If you had been standing on an open deck on a foggy morning, you probably would have smelled the sea lions before you saw them.

Later, the catamaran nosed onto an isolated gravel shore to deposit a team of kayaker-campers, which included a husband and wife celebrating their twenty-fifth wedding anniversary in the wilderness paradise where they first met. We picked up groups of kayakers, too, all of them reluctant to end the adventure of their lives. During their paddling and camping trips, the kayakers had seen several bears. One party had even paddled quietly past brown bear mothers and their cubs prying mussels

from the rocks for a low-tide lunch. Bears in Southeast Alaska have traditionally been hunted along shores and beaches, but those within the park boundaries are protected. As a result, they've become somewhat accustomed to finding humans in their habitat. This makes it much easier to see bears when visiting the park, but anyone on foot must exercise extreme caution.

From the boat deck, we spotted a black bear and several brown (grizzly) bears. We also saw some mountain goats—quite a surprise at sea level. One was even wading in Tarr Inlet, seemingly imitating a nearby bear, nibbling at sea grasses that had washed ashore.

Within the boundaries of Glacier Bay National Park and Preserve are five major land ecosystems: wet tundra, or muskeg; coastal western hemlock and Sitka spruce forest; alpine tundra; glaciers and ice fields; and early post-glacial meadows and thickets. Add to those three marine ecosystems: the continental shelf, wave-beaten coasts, and fjord estuaries. Only the edges of the bay and the coastal forests see many human visitors.

Glacier Bay is a unique laboratory for professional researchers, but even lay people in a one- or two-day visit can come away with an understanding of the park's fascinating geology, ecosystems, glaciology, and how the land regenerates after glaciers retreat. A park naturalist joins every ship entering the bay, interpreting in nonscientific language the marine and on-shore ecosystems for park visitors.

Although a resident of steep mountainsides, the mountain goat often browses near tidewater.

The park is home to about 420 species of plants. Carried from far away by the wind and birds, the seeds and spores of the most adaptable plants are always the first to grow on the ground that is exposed by the retreating glaciers. Mosses, algae, and lichen form a blanket on which succeeding plants can take root. Horsetail, dwarf fireweed, dryas, and willow are among the pioneer plants. The nitrogen-fixing alder comes next, and then cottonwood trees. Eventually stands of Sitka spruce and western hemlock, with an undergrowth of devil's club, replace the alder thickets and cottonwoods. At the Bartlett Cove area, which was the first ice-free zone in Glacier Bay, the conifers have grown into a mature rain forest. Walking there in the silence and dampness, listening to the song of a winter wren, is a great contrast to being around the grinding, crunching glaciers.

While birds, flying insects, and marine creatures recolonized Glacier Bay quickly, it has taken land mammals longer to establish themselves. The highly mobile brown bears and mountain goats returned first and are thriving. But only recently have moose, coyotes, and wolves appeared. Among the forty mammal species in the park and preserve are the redbacked vole, red squirrel, porcupine, hoary marmot, marten, mink, and wolverine. Keep an eye out for the one amphibian, the boreal toad. Sitka blacktailed deer live on Chichagof Island just across Icy Strait and have been sighted in some areas of Glacier Bay.

Hike the trails in the Bartlett Cove area, and you might meet a raven, brown creeper, hermit thrush, woodpecker, and, in spring, a male blue grouse displaying. Or

A family of mallard ducklings rest beside a rain forest pond.

walk any shoreline between the rain forest and high-tide line to discover another cast of creatures in the sedge and beach wildflowers: a coyote hunting birds or mice, a bear (or, more likely, its tracks), a rufous hummingbird sampling the wild blossoms, a golden-crowned sparrow, even an American robin. It's a wonderful way to walk off an extravagant breakfast or to watch a golden sunset.

It is fitting that the marine mammals that have come to symbolize the struggle to preserve natural habitat have found sanctuary in Glacier Bay. Populations of the fast-swimming minke whale are shrinking everywhere, but a few shy ones visit Glacier Bay. Glacier Bay's humpback whales are much more visible, which is understandable for mammals that weigh in at thirty-two tons and average forty to fifty feet in length. The park's humpbacks winter in Hawaii and summer in Glacier Bay, where they feed on the abundant krill, herring, and capelin.

To see the humpbacks' twisting leaps, or breaches, and witness their fascinating bubble-net–feeding techniques at close range is an experience of a lifetime. On one wildlife-viewing trip, the bay suddenly seemed to boil all around our boat. Somewhere below us a group of humpbacks had encircled a school of herring in a "net" of bubbles, using their unique cooperative-feeding method to entrap the prey. Suddenly the whales exploded on the surface, gorging on the small fish and drenching us and our cameras in the process. How could anyone forget a moment like that?

For many the orca, or killer whale, is the glamour queen of Glacier Bay. The orca has no natural enemies and feeds on squid, fish, seals and sea lions, porpoises, sharks, and whales. Seeing an orca actually catching its dinner is unusual, however. The six-foot-high dorsal fin of an old male slicing through the water on a calm morning is a more likely orca sighting, and you'll see more than one, as the highly social orcas travel in groups, called pods. Dall porpoises appear occasionally in the bay and at a distance can be mistaken for orcas, though the orca is on average three times larger. The smaller harbor porpoises are a far more frequent sight.

Sea otter sightings can't be predicted—some days the otters seem shy; on other days, these appealing animals can be closely observed. One morning, while aboard a small sightseeing boat, I saw a young otter floating alone on the water's surface. *An orca must have captured its mother*, I thought. Just then, the mother popped to the surface, grabbed the baby by the neck, and dragged it below to safety.

The pine marten is at home in the older coastal forests of Glacier Bay.

slabs of glacial ice—pan ice—that calve into the inlet are ideal and safe islands for seals to give birth.

Even in a national park where the tidewater glaciers, marine mammals, seabirds, and the pure grandeur of the long summer days are the primary magnets, serious birders and anglers won't be disappointed. In a week's time a birder might tick off half of the 223 avian species, especially during spring and fall migrations. Sport anglers will find salmon, halibut, lingcod, and cutthroat and Dolly Varden trout.

One of Glacier Bay's most spectacular inlets, the ice-choked approach to Johns Hopkins Glacier, with its seven-thousand-foot-high rock walls, is closed to all visitors early each summer while the harbor seals whelp. Pups born on shore are vulnerable to bear attacks, so the large

Glacier Bay National Park and Preserve is about forty-five miles from Juneau, Alaska's capital. No highways connect the park to the "outside" world, nor does the busy Alaska Marine Highway system stop there, so at one time Glacier Bay was not a convenient destination. In 1953, however, a pioneering cruise ship line brought its passengers into the area. The voyages were so popular that by 1960 other cruise lines followed suit. Now about 80 to 90 percent of the park's visitors—360,000 people a year—arrive by oceangoing liners, some of them the largest and most luxurious vessels in operation. The ships provide a comfortable, hassle-free way for the passengers to view a global wonder.

From Gustavus it is ten miles by paved road (the *only* road in Glacier Bay National Park) to Bartlett Cove and the snug, rustic Glacier Bay Lodge, park headquarters, and land's end in a lush green rain forest. From the visitors' center in the lodge, rangers lead daily hikes—rain or shine—on a network of forest trails and offer natural and cultural history programs each evening. Strong walkers will enjoy the eight-mile round-trip hike to Bartlett Lake, a rich adventure in a mossy world where moose sightings are common.

For more than a hundred miles from Cape Spencer to Cape Fairweather and beyond to Dry Bay, the outer coast of Glacier Bay National Park and Preserve is uninhabited and unprotected from the frequent savage storms that roll in from the Gulf of Alaska. Only one bay, Lituya, site of Cenotaph Island, offers shelter.

In 1990, my wife, Peggy, and I visited one of the most remote sections of Glacier Bay National Park. We boarded inflatable rafts near Haines Junction, Yukon Territory, for a float trip down the pristine Alsek River through Kluane National Park, British Columbia's Tatshenshini Park, and finally into Glacier Bay. After almost two weeks of snow squalls followed by sunshine,

plunging through whitewater rapids, and tenting at night, we arrived at tidewater: Dry Bay, on the Gulf of Alaska, where the park ranger who met us was also the U.S. immigration officer.

The Alsek may be the world's premier wild river, racing through one of the largest surviving wildernesses. En route we saw no humans and no dwellings other than a dilapidated trapper's shack. What we did see were stupendous scenery, glaciers calving into the river, and wildlife—wolves, mountain goats, waterfowl, a wolverine, eagles, shorebirds, geese, and bears, bears, bears. Most of the bears had the distinctive shoulder hump of the grizzly, but one had a strange, smoky blue coat, a rare color phase of the Alaskan black bear. This glacier bear is unique to this beautiful park and preserve and the area just northwest toward Yakutat.

In 1982, Glacier Bay National Park and Preserve, together with Alaska's Wrangell-St. Elias National Park, and Canada's Kluane National Park and Tatshenshini-Alsek Provincial Park, became a twenty-four-million-acre world heritage site, the largest internationally protected area in the world. In 1986, UNESCO, the United Nations Educational, Scientific, and Cultural

Organization, designated the park and preserve (along with Admiralty Island National Monument) as a biosphere reserve. Those designations and the scientific and cultural significance of Glacier Bay would seem to guarantee its protection from exploitation forever.

Not to protect this remarkable place, a magnificent land still emerging from an ice age, would be the world's loss.

LEFT: *Playful river otters are often seen along Glacier Bay shorelines.*

RIGHT: *Every spring, nesting gulls and cormorants claim and occupy the small islands of Glacier Bay.*

Retreating glaciers expose bare rock slopes in Johns Hopkins Inlet.
The icebergs are a couple centuries old.

LEFT: *The slick underside of a recently overturned iceberg looks strange and beautiful in early dawn light.*

BELOW: *Bergs, like this giant, break away from tidewater glacier faces and drift slowly, melting, toward the mouth of Glacier Bay.*

RIGHT: *Huge chunks of ice are ready to break away from the steep face of Reid Glacier.*

FAR LEFT: *The east shore of South Marble Island is a traditional, multicolored haulout of Steller's sea lions.*

LEFT: *The bellowing of sea lions jostling for space on South Marble Island can be heard even before they come into the view of passing boats.*

BELOW: *From their secure, protected base, sea lions hunt widely over Glacier Bay to feed on shrimp, squid, and fish—especially cod and herring.*

FAR LEFT: *Dramatically shaped icebergs serve as convenient resting places for gulls and other foraging seabirds.*

LEFT: *Often huge bergs are blown aground and then slowly melt.*

BELOW: *Orcas, or killer whales, are elusive. Some days they are easy to spot travelling or cavorting on the surface; other days they keep out of sight.*

ABOVE: *Pigeon guillemots are year-round residents of
Glacier Bay.*

RIGHT: *Tufted puffins courting. They will nest in burrows on
sea cliffs and steep rocky or rubble slopes.*

FAR RIGHT: *Because they are so striking in appearance,
tufted puffins are easily spotted by birders.*

LEFT: *A late afternoon sun illuminates the wild outer coast of Glacier Bay National Park.*

RIGHT: *Present every summer in coastal forests, the Northern Goshawk is an elusive but sought-after sighting for birders.*

LEFT: *On a cool morning the green rain forest is perfectly reflected in a pool along a hiking trail near Bartlett Cove.*

ABOVE: *Rock sandpipers are commonly seen in flocks when migrating through the park; this lone sandpiper is an unusual sight.*

RIGHT: *Bright green leaves of devil's club hide the prickly stems of this forest shrub, which later will bear cone-shaped clusters of red berries.*

LEFT: *Forget-me-not is a colorful early summer wildflower.*

BELOW: *The crimson flowers found on beaches or in open meadows are coastal paintbrushes.*

RIGHT: *A miniature member of the dogwood family, bunchberry is a resident of forests and muskeg in Southeast Alaska.*

LEFT: *In the extreme western area of the park, Alsek Glacier melts into the Alsek River and finally into remote Dry Bay.*

RIGHT: *Fall meadows of soapberries along the Alsek River attract grizzly bears and many smaller mammals.*

LEFT: *The rhinoceros auklet is a very rare sighting in the park.*

BELOW: *The sometimes noisy Steller's jay is a year-round resident of coastal, coniferous woodlands.*

RIGHT: *From late spring until late fall, the red-throated loon is one of the four loon species commonly found at Glacier Bay.*

LEFT: *Waters of Glacier Bay's long coastline teem with marine life such as this hermit crab.*

ABOVE: *Predators of mussels and smaller organisms, multi-tentacled green anemones are exposed by low tides.*

RIGHT: *Purple sea urchins especially thrive along the windy outer coast where wave action is strongest.*

LEFT: *A melting iceberg drifts slowly along the steep shore near Tlingit Point. It will never reach the open water of Icy Strait.*

RIGHT: *The low sun of early morning or late evening gives the floating icebergs of Glacier Bay an unearthly glow.*

ABOVE: *The nutritious new grasses of spring that grow along shorelines attract brown bears such as this female and cub.*

RIGHT: *Footprints in tidal muck indicate that a brown bear recently passed this way.*

FAR RIGHT: *Brown bears may be encountered anywhere along the shores of Glacier Bay.*

LEFT: *By far the most acrobatic of whales, humpbacks can heave their heavy bodies above Glacier Bay's surface.*

RIGHT: *What goes up must come down: a humpback whale tail waves to the camera.*

LEFT: *An alder grows from a decaying fallen tree trunk in the lush rain forest near Bartlett Cove.*

RIGHT: *Never an easy animal to observe anywhere, the stealthy lynx is rarely glimpsed in Glacier Bay. Your best chance for a lynx sighting occurs along the Alsek River drainage.*

LEFT: *Harbor seals are common in Glacier Bay National Park.*

RIGHT: *This adult harbor seal lolls in sunshine on a small iceberg.*

LEFT: *The spots of bright yellow color along Glacier Bay's remote Alsek River belong to the coastal paintbrush, common throughout Southeast Alaska.*

BELOW: *Yellow paintbrush blooms in summer on a lonely coastal beach.*

RIGHT: *Every spring the new, butter-colored spathes of skunk cabbage grow in Glacier Bay's boggiest places. Many creatures, including beetles, bears, and geese, dine on the plant.*

LEFT: *Peaks of the St. Elias mountain range loom over the western-most portion of the park.*

RIGHT: *A mother brown bear with a cub explores the steep shore, probably to forage for mussels.*

ABOVE: *Once nearly hunted to extinction, sea otters thrive today in Glacier Bay. This one cracks and eats clams.*

RIGHT: *An adult sea otter surfaces with a sea urchin.*

FAR RIGHT: *Two mature otters groom in the cold Alaskan current.*

LEFT: *More likely heard than seen, wolves are occasionally encountered along the shores of Glacier Bay.*

RIGHT: *The number of wolves that experience dark color phases is much greater in Southeast Alaska than elsewhere; sightings of all-black individuals have been reported in Glacier Bay.*

LEFT: *Black-legged kittiwakes nest in colonies, often on steep cliff faces of Glacier Bay, where they are numerous every summer.*

ABOVE: *A pelagic gull, most black-legged kittiwakes forage out across the Gulf of Alaska in winter.*

RIGHT: *Black-legged kittiwakes, glacous-winged gulls, and mew gulls share summertime resting and nesting islands with pelagic cormorants.*

LEFT: *About 5,000 pairs of mature bald eagles live in southeastern Alaska today, with varying numbers in Glacier Bay.*

RIGHT: *An adult bald eagle with young to feed flies from its treetop nest on a fishing expedition near Bartlett Cove.*

Tons of ice fall into the bay from Margerie Glacier, one of nine tidewater glaciers. This explosive calving goes on day and night.

LEFT: *Bergs from calving glaciers serve as resting places for harbor seals.*

RIGHT: *Steller's sea lions hauling out on South Marble Island.*

LEFT: *A male rufous hummingbird provides a brilliant focus of color near Glacier Bay Lodge. These hummers are regular summer visitors here.*

RIGHT: *In July a common redpoll remains motionless in its tree nest.*

ABOVE: *As if to celebrate summer, purple wild irises bloom in scattered places: in meadows, open woodlands, and damp roadsides.*

RIGHT: *Small shooting stars are among the most exquisite and widespread wildflowers of Glacier Bay. These grace the area near Bartlett Cove.*

FAR RIGHT: *This garden of Nootka lupine grows near Glacier Bay Lodge. The roots were once harvested, roasted, and eaten by Tlingit Indians.*

On many mornings, even in glorious summer, the arms of Glacier Bay are shrouded in mist and fog, making the stark shapes and colors of floating icebergs more vivid than in bright sunlight.

FAR LEFT: *A rare visitor to Glacier Bay, this bluewinged teal drake flushes suddenly from a quiet pond.*

LEFT: *A walk along a Bartlett Cove beach reveals this short-eared owl.*

BELOW: *A migrating yellowlegs pauses on a Glacier Bay shore to rest, balanced on one leg.*

LEFT: *This red-breasted merganser female is one of thousands that winter along the Southeast Alaska coast.*

BELOW: *A bald eagle finds a fish that washed ashore in Beartrack Cove. Soon other eagles will come to share the feast.*

RIGHT: *Snowy mountains loom everywhere in the park landscape.*

LEFT: *A sleek mammal's head quietly breaks the surface, then turns to take in the view—it is a harbor seal.*

ABOVE: *From the beach, a seal inspects a party of kayakers passing nearby.*

RIGHT: *These harbor seals seem to debate whether the kayakers are friend or foe.*

From any distance the face of Margerie Glacier is a splendid sight.

Published by Sasquatch Books
Printed in Hong Kong
Distributed in Canada by Raincoast Books, Ltd.
04 03 02 01 01   5 4 3 2 1

Cover and interior design: Karen Schober
Map and interior illustrations: Linda Feltner

Library of Congress Cataloging in Publication Data
Bauer, Erwin A.
   Glacier Bay : the wild beauty of Glacier Bay National Park / by Erwin
& Peggy Bauer.
          p. cm.
   ISBN 1-57061-210-2 (alk. paper)
1. Glacier Bay National Park and Preserve (Alaska)—Pictorial works. 2.
Natural history—Alaska—Glacier Bay National Park and Preserve—
Pictorial works. I. Bauer, Peggy. II. Title.
F912.G5 B38 2000
508.798'2'0222—dc21 00-029694

Sasquatch Books
615 Second Avenue
Seattle, Washington 98104
(206) 467-4300
www.SasquatchBooks.com
books@SasquatchBooks.com

Glacier Bay National Park and Preserve
P.O. Box 140
Gustavus, Alaska 99826
907/697-2627 (summer); 907/697-2230 (winter)
907/697-2406 (summer fax); 907/697-2654 (winter fax)
www.nps.gov/glba/

Established in 1925 as a national monument, the park was expanded and designated a marine wilderness area in 1980 when it became 3.3-million-acre Glacier Bay National Park and Preserve. In addition to the spectacular glaciers and icebergs—about one-quarter of the region is under ice—the park encompasses breathtaking peaks and mountain ranges, dynamic wildlife, forests, tundra, valleys, beaches, islands, and fjords.

Although the park is open year-round, the peak season for visiting Glacier Bay is from mid-May to mid-September, with July being the most popular and active month. The best way to enjoy the park is on the water, and ninety percent of visitors see it from one of the many cruise ships that ply the bay. Other visitors arrive via chartered flights, private boats (permit required), or by daily air service and passenger ferries operating between Juneau and Gustavus. A small, tidy community of several hundred year-round residents, Gustavus accommodates Glacier Bay tourists with everything from lodging, food, guiding, medical, and transportation services to kayak and fishing tackle rentals. Summer activities include boat tours, camping (backcountry permits required), sea kayaking, fishing, rafting, and attending ranger naturalist programs.

The park headquarters and Visitor Center are located on Bartlett Cove, about ten miles by road beyond Gustavus, and provide boating and backcountry permits, information on accessible day hikes, and schedules for ranger-led activities. There is also a giftshop, featuring Glacier Bay and Alaska titles, and the Glacier Bay Lodge, 800/451-5952, that offers overnight accommodations and popular boat tours (reservations recommended) in summer.

SELECT BIBLIOGRAPHY

Bauer, Erwin. *Wild Alaska.* New York: Outdoor Life Books, 1988.

Corral, Kim, Hannah, and Roy. *A Child's Glacier Bay.* Portland, Oregon: Alaska Northwest Books, 1998.

DuFresne, Jim. *Glacier Bay National Park: A Backcountry Guide to the Glaciers and Beyond.* Seattle: Mountaineers Books, 1987.

Elliot, Nan. *Best Places Alaska.* Seattle: Sasquatch Books, 2000.

Howard, Jim. *Guide to Sea Kayaking in Southeast Alaska: The Best Trips and Tours from Misty Fjords to Glacier Bay.* Old Saybrook, Connecticut: Globe Pequot, 1999.

Jettmar, Karen. *Alaska's Glacier Bay: A Traveler's Guide.* Portland, Oregon: Alaska Northwest Books, 1997.

Muir, John. *Travels in Alaska.* New York: Houghton Mifflin, 1998 (reissue).

Pine marten

Based on the Olympic Peninsula of Washington State, Erwin and Peggy Bauer

are considered two of the world's premier wildlife photographers. A prolific husband-and-wife

team—with half a million images in their photo file—the Bauers' photographs have appeared in

nature magazines around the globe and graced more than 300 published covers. Together they have

produced 45 books on wildlife and the outdoors. While the Bauers continue to travel all over the

world to photograph animals and landscapes, they have developed a special relationship with

Alaska in the last 25 years, where they return again and again. They are also the recipients

of many awards, including most recently the prestigious North American Nature

Photography Association's 2000 Lifetime Achievement Award.